Star of the Empress

(*Sitāra-e-Qaiṣarah*)

By

Ḥaḍrat Mirzā Ghulām Aḥmad

*The Promised Messiah and Mahdi,
Founder of the Aḥmadiyya Muslim Jamāʿat,
on whom be peace*

ISLAM INTERNATIONAL PUBLICATIONS LTD.
TILFORD, SURREY, UNITED KINGDOM

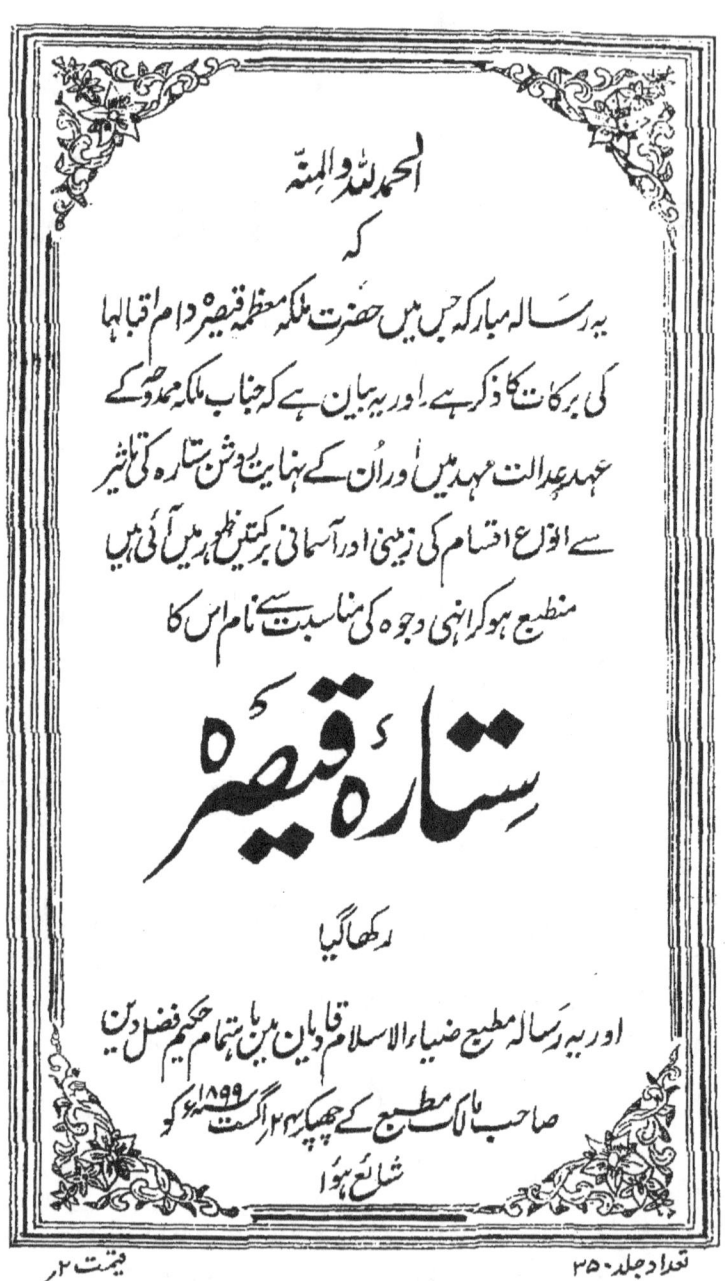

Facsimile of the original Urdu title page printed in 1899

*All Praise belongs to Allah;
it is to Him that we offer gratitude*

This auspicious booklet cites the blessings of Her Majesty, the Empress, may her prosperity endure, and mentions that in the time of Her Majesty's tranquil reign and due to the influence of her resplendent star, countless earthly and heavenly blessings have been manifested.

Let it be known that in keeping with these reasons, the following booklet has been entitled:

Star of the Empress

Published at Ḍiyāul-Islām Press, Qadian
under the supervision of Ḥakīm Faḍl Dīn,
Proprietor of the Press, on
24 August 1899

350 Copies Printed   Price: 2 Annas

Translation of the original Urdu title page.

Star of the Empress

An English rendering of *Sitāra-e-Qaiṣarah*,
written by Ḥaḍrat Mirzā Ghulām Aḥmad,
The Promised Messiah and Mahdi, on whom be peace,
Founder of the Aḥmadiyya Muslim Jamāʿat

Translated from Urdu into English by: Sharmeen Butt
Revised by: Ayyaz Mahmood Khan

First published in Urdu in Qadian, India: 1899
First English translation published in UK: 2013

© Islam International Publications Ltd.

Published by
Islam International Publications Ltd.
Islamabad, Sheephatch Lane
Tilford, Surrey GU10 2AQ, UK

Printed in UK at
Raqeem Press, Tilford, UK

For further information please contact:
Ahmadiyya Muslims Association UK
Baitul-Futuh, 181 London Road,
Morden, Surrey, SM4 5PT
Tel: +44 (0) 20 8687 7800
or visit www.alislam.org.

ISBN: 978-1-84880-086-1

CONTENTS

About the Author .... *vii*
Foreword .... *ix*

Text of Sitāra-e-Qaiṣarah 1

An Important Note *19*
Glossary *23*
Index *27*

ABOUT THE AUTHOR

Ḥaḍrat Mirzā Ghulām Aḥmad[as] was born in 1835 in Qadian, India. From his early life, he dedicated himself to prayer, and the study of the Holy Quran as well as other scriptures. He was deeply pained to observe the plight of Islam which was being attacked from all directions. In order to defend Islam and present its teachings in their pristine purity, he wrote ninety-one books, thousands of letters, and participated in many religious debates. He argued that Islam is a living faith which can lead man to establish communion with God and achieve moral and spiritual perfection.

Ḥaḍrat Mirzā Ghulām Aḥmad[as] started experiencing divine dreams, visions and revelations at a young age. This communication from God continued to increase and he announced that God had appointed him to be the same Reformer of the latter days as prophesied by various religions under different titles. He also claimed to be the Promised Messiah and Mahdi whose advent had been prophesied by the Holy Prophet Muḥammad (may the peace and blessing of Allah be upon him). In 1889, under divine command, he started accepting initiation into the Ahmadiyya

Muslim Community, which is now established in more than 200 countries.

After his demise in 1908, the institution of *khilāfat* was established to succeed him in fulfillment of the prophecy made in the Holy Quran that Allah the Almighty would establish *khilāfat* (successorship) among the Muslims. Ḥaḍrat Mirza Masroor Ahmad[aba] is the Fifth Successor to the Promised Messiah[as] and the present head of the Ahmadiyya Muslim Community.

FOREWORD

The book *Sitāra-e-Qaiṣarah* [Star of the Empress] was written by the Promised Messiah[as] on 20 August 1899 and published on 24 August 1899. In this brief exposition, the Promised Messiah[as] has presented, in a new light, the same views expressed in his book *Tohfa-e-Qaiṣariyyah* [A Gift for the Queen], which was written on the occasion of the Diamond Jubilee of Her Majesty, Queen Victoria. In this book, the Promised Messiah[as] has once again commended the British government for granting peace, security and religious freedom to all its subjects. He has then refuted the false doctrine of the advent of a militant Messiah and Mahdi, who according to some, would presumably, coerce the world into accepting Islam. Furthermore, he has also beautifully removed misconceptions surrounding the concept of Jihad and clearly expounds that Islam was never spread by the sword, nor is religious compulsion permitted in Islam. The Promised Messiah[as] then goes on to beautifully explain that the Christian concept of atonement, which logically results in Jesus[as] bearing the burden of curse, is a dishonour to the pure and holy person of Jesus[as]. Finally, the Promised Messiah[as] has presented his claim as being the Promised Messiah and Mahdi of the latter days, awaited by all world religions.

In 2012, on the auspicious occasion of the Diamond Jubilee of Her Majesy, Queen Elizabeth II, the Ahmadiyya Muslim Community published the English translation of *Tohfa-e-Qaiṣariyyah* [A Gift for the Queen]. Now, Allah the Exalted has enabled us to publish the English translation of *Sitāra-e-Qaiṣarah* [Star of the Empress]. The Ahmadiyya Muslim Community was established in the United Kingdom in 1913 and had the honour of building London's first ever mosque, known as the Fazl Mosque or the London Mosque.

This book was translated from Urdu into English by Sharmeen Butt and the initial review was done by Mohamed Arshad Ahmedi. The text was revised and prepared for print by Ayyaz Mahmood Khan. May Allah the Exalted reward them all abundantly. *Āmīn*.

Munir-ud-Din Shams
Additional Vakīlut-Taṣnīf
London, United Kingdom
April 2013

TO THE MAGNIFICENT QUEEN, HER MAJESTY, THE EMPRESS OF INDIA & ENGLAND

MAY ALLAH MAKE HER PROSPERITY ENDURE!

First and foremost, I pray that may the God of Omnipotence immensely bless the life of Her Majesty, the Queen of India, and increase her in prosperity, in rank and grandeur, and grant her the delight of her eyes by affording security to her sons and dear ones. After this, the writer of this submission, **Mirzā Ghulām Aḥmad of Qadian**, who lives in a small village of the Punjab named **Qadian**; which is situated approximately seventy miles from Lahore in the northeast corner of the district of Gurdaspur, submits that in general, most inhabitants of this country possess emotions of apposite love and sincere obedience for Her Majesty, may her prosperity endure, according to their individual degrees of perception, insight and gratitude. This stems from the comforts they are enjoying due to Her Majesty, the Queen of India's sense of fairness for all, benevolence to her subjects and administration of justice; and also on account of those peace policies and plans for the wellbeing of her subjects of all social strata, which have materalised at the expense of millions of rupees and through immeasurable generosity. There is the exception of a small minority of people, who I believe, also exist in hiding and live like savages and beasts. However, due to the understanding and knowledge that I possess in relation to the rights owed to this noble government and which I have already expounded in my book *'Tohfa-e-Qaiṣariyyah,'* [A Gift for the Queen] this humble one holds such a high degree of sincerity, love and fervour of obedience for Her Majesty and for her noble officials that I do not have the words with which to express this sincerity. Enthused by this very true affection and sincerity, on the celebration of the 'Sixtieth Jubilee' I wrote a book addressed to Her Majesty, the Empress of India, may her prosperity endure. I entitled it *'Tohfa-e-Qaiṣariyyah,'* [A Gift for the Queen] and dispatched it as a humble gift to Her Majesty. I was most certain that I would be honoured with a response and that this would be a source of my exaltation beyond expectation. The basis of this hope and certainty were the high moral standards of Her Majesty, the Empress of India, which are renowned in all the countries of the East and like Her Majesty's kingdom, are so unparalleled in their extent and breadth, that it is impossible to find their similitude anywhere else. Nevertheless, I am extremely surprised that I was not even obliged with a single royal word. My conscience does not accept on any account that if my humble offering, that is, the book *'Tohfa-e-Qaiṣariyyah,'* [A Gift for the Queen] had been presented to Her Majesty, the Empress, I would not have been obliged with a reply. Most certainly there must be some other reason which has nothing to do with the will, choice and knowledge of Her Majesty, the Empress of India, may her prosperity endure. Hence, the favourable view that I hold for Her Majesty, has compelled me once again to draw the attention of Her Majesty towards this gift, that is, *Toḥfa-e-Qaiṣariyyah,* [A Gift for the Queen] so that I may derive joy from a few words of royal approval. **It is for this purpose that I dispatch this submission.** I hereby venture to submit a few words to Her Majesty, the Honoured Empress of India, may her prosperity endure. I belong to a noble Mughal family of the Punjab and prior to the Sikh reign; my ancestors were rulers of an independent State. My great-grandfather **Mirzā Gul Muḥammad** was such a wise, sagacious, valiant and virtuous person with skills of governance that when the sovereignty of the Chughtā'ī kings of Delhi fell weak, due to their inability, decadence, indolence, and lack of determination, certain courtiers undertook efforts for him to ascend the throne of Delhi. For he possessed all the characteristics associated with intelligence and benevolence for his subjects, and he was also from a royal family. However, since the fate and reign of the kings of Delhi was all but consumed, this proposal did not gain widespread approval. Many atrocities were committed against us during the reign of the Sikhs and our ancestors were evicted from all the villages of the State. Not a moment was spent in peace. Our entire State was mixed to dust before the auspicious rule of the British could step in and only five villages remained. My father, the late Mirzā Ghulām Murtaḍā, who had faced great misfortunes during the reign of the Sikhs awaited the British rule like a thirsty person who longs for water. When the British government assumed rule of this country, he was so overjoyed by this blessing, i.e., by the establishment of the British government, that it was as if he had discovered a treasure-trove. He was a great well-wisher and devotee of the British government. It is for this reason that he provided fifty mounted horses to the British government as assistance, during the mutiny of 1857. Even afterwards, he always remained vigilant so that if his assistance was ever required, he would most willingly afford it to this government. Had the mutiny of 1857 went on any further, he was prepared to provide the help of up to an additional hundred cavalry-men. In short, this is the manner in which his life was spent. After his demise, this humble one detached himself completely from worldly matters and became occupied with God the Exalted. The service that I have rendered in support of the British government is that I arranged for the publication of a quantity of approximately fifty thousand books, journals and posters, which were then distributed throughout the country as well as in other Islamic countries. These were published on the subject that the British government is a well-wisher for us, the Muslims; therefore, it should be the obligation of each and every Muslim to be truly obedient to this government and be sincerely grateful for this good fortune and continue to supplicate for it. I wrote these books in various languages, namely, Urdu, Persian and Arabic, and distributed them throughout the Muslim world, so much so that they were even published widely throughout Makkah and Madīnah, the two sacred cities of Islam. Moreover, they were distributed in Constantinople, the capital of the Byzantine Empire; in Syria, Egypt, Kabul and in other cities of Afghanistan insofar as possible. As a result, hundreds of thousands of people gave up their false notions on Jihad, which had taken root in their hearts due to the teachings of ignorant

Mullahs. I take pride in the fact that no other Muslim in British India was able to match the service, which came to pass through me. I do not deem this twenty-two year service of mine as being a favour upon this benevolent government. For I acknowledge that with the coming of this government, we and our ancestors, were delivered from a burning iron furnace. It is for this reason that along with all my dear ones, I raise my hands and supplicate; O God, keep this august Empress of India, may her sovereignty endure, safe and may she reign long over us, and let the shade of Your succour protect her at every step, and prolong the days of her prosperity.

These were the circumstances, services and prayers that I earlier submitted in *'Toḥfa-e-Qaiṣariyyah,'* [A Gift for the Queen] which was sent to Her Majesty, the Empress of India. In view of Her Majesty's innumerable moral qualities, every day I remained hopeful to receive a reply and I continue to maintain this hope. I believe it is impossible that if the humble gift of a well-wisher such as myself, which was [a book] written with immense sincerity from the depth of my heart, had been presented to Her Majesty, the Empress of India, may her prosperity endure, it would not have brought forth a response. On the contrary, indeed, it would have arrived; indeed, it would have arrived. Therefore, I am compelled to write this submission as a reminder, due to the immense confidence I hold in the gracious morals of the Empress of India. This submission is not a mere composition of the pen; rather, my heart has compelled the hand to write this letter of goodwill with the strength of certainty. I pray that God the Exalted may cause this letter to reach Her Majesty, the Empress of

India, may her prosperity endure, at a time of peace, security and joy. Furthermore, that He inspires the heart of Her Majesty to recognise with her pure insight, the true affection and sincerity that I have in my heart for her revered self, and she, by virtue of her benevolence, obliges me with a considerate reply. I have also been commissioned to convey the glad tidings to Her Majesty, the magnificent Empress of India, that just as on earth and through worldly means, God the Exalted, with His infinite Mercy and perfect Wisdom has established the rule of Her Majesty in this country and abroad, so that He may fill the world with justice and peace; similarly, from the unseen, He has Himself ordained in Heaven, the establishment of a spiritual system in her auspicious reign, so that the heart-felt objectives of our august Queen, the Empress of India, may be fulfilled and supported, which are to promote justice, peace and the welfare of mankind; the eradication of disorder, reformation of morals and the removal of savage conditions. This shall nurture with heavenly water the garden of peace, security and goodwill that she wishes to plant. In accordance with His eternal promise with respect to the advent of the Promised Messiah, He has sent me from Heaven, so that in the spirit of that man of God, who was born in Bethlehem and brought up in Nazareth, I may engage myself in assisting with the good and blessed objectives of Her Majesty. He has anointed me with countless blessings and has appointed me as His Messiah so that from Heaven, He may Himself support Her Majesty in her pure ambitions. O Blessed Empress, may God protect you and gladden our hearts with your long life, prosperity and success. The advent of the Promised Messiah in your reign, which is filled with the light of sincerity, is a testimony from God that you excel all other monarchs in your love for peace, good governance, compassion towards your subjects and in justice and equity. Both Muslims and Christians believe in the forthcoming advent of the Promised Messiah. However, they state that he shall appear in an era and time when the wolf and lamb will feed together and children will play with serpents. Thus, O august Empress, this refers to your era and your reign. One who has eyes may see and one who is free from prejudice, may understand. Your Majesty, it is your reign alone which has gathered beasts and meek birds in one place. The honest, who are like children, interact with mischievous serpents and they have no fear under your peaceful patronage. Which other reign could be more peaceful than yours in which the Promised Messiah would come? O august Empress, your pure ambitions draw in Divine succour and due to the magnetism of your good intentions the Heaven continues to lean towards the earth with mercy. Hence, there is no other reign other than your own which would be appropriate for the advent of the Promised Messiah. Thus, God has sent down a light from the Heavens during your luminous era, because light draws in light while darkness attracts darkness. O august and honourable Queen of the age, clear indications of your peaceful reign are found in the books which allude to the advent of the Promised Messiah. However, it was essential for the Promised Messiah to appear in the world just as Īliyā [Prophet Elijah] came as a manifestation of Yūhannā [John the Baptist]; that is, in his essence and disposition, Yūhannā became Īliyā in the sight of God. The same happened here, in that a person has been vested with the essence and disposition of ʿĪsā [Jesus] (on whom be peace) in your blessed era. This is why he has been named the Messiah. His advent was certain because it is not possible for God's holy scriptures of the past to prove false. Your Majesty, O Pride of all her subjects, it is the custom of God since time immemorial that if the sovereign of the time is well-intentioned and desires the welfare of his subjects; when in accordance with his power, he has fully instituted a system for public peace and goodness, and his heart is empathetic for the public to make pious transformations, Divine mercy becomes ebullient for him in Heaven. A spiritual man is sent to earth according to the [sovereign's] strength and desire. The birth of such a perfect reformer is brought about by the pure-intent, courage and universal sympathy of that just ruler. This comes to pass when an equitable ruler is born as an earthly saviour, and owing to his extraordinary courage and sympathy for mankind, he naturally requires a heavenly saviour. This is what occurred at the time of the Messiah (on whom be peace), because Caesar, the Roman Emperor of that time was a good person and was averse to cruelty on earth. Moreover, he sought the welfare and salvation of the people. It was then that the God of Heaven raised a light-giving moon from the land of Nazareth - 'Īsā [Jesus], the Messiah; so that just as the word *'Nazareth'* signifies verdure, freshness and greenery in Hebrew, the same could be instilled in the hearts of people. O our dear Empress of India, may God grant you long life. Your goodness of intent and sincere sympathy for your subjects is no less than that of the Caesar of Rome. In fact, we forcefully state that it is far greater than his because there is a multitude of poor subjects under you, with whom Your Majesty wishes to be sympathetic. The manner in which you desire the benefit of your humble subjects in every respect, and the manner in which you have demonstrated examples of your philanthropy and benevolence to your subjects, are such excellent qualities and blessings as are not found in any of the previous monarchs. Therefore, your works, which are completely imbued with goodness and beneficence, above all require that just as Your Majesty is compassionate about the salvation, welfare and comfort of all your subjects and as you are engaged in initiatives for benevolence towards your subjects, God in Heaven too, may assist you. Therefore, this Promised Messiah who has come to the world is but one outcome of your blessed person, sincere good intention and true sympathy. During your reign God has remembered the grieved people of the world and He has sent His Messiah from Heaven. He was born in your kingdom and in your empire so that this may serve as a testimony to the world that the dispensation of justice in your dominion has attracted the dispensation of justice in Heaven towards itself. Your dispensation of grace has generated a dispensation of grace in Heaven. As the coming of this Messiah serves as a final judgement in the world on the distinction between truth and falsehood, it is for this reason that the Promised Messiah is called *Ḥakam* [Arbiter]. Just as the word *'Nazareth'* alludes to an era of freshness and verdure, the village of this Messiah was called Islāmpūr Qāḍī Mājhī. In this manner, the word *'Qāḍī'* [Judge] could make an indication towards the final Arbiter of God, through whom God's chosen ones would be given the glad-tiding of eternal grace. Furthermore, this would also serve as a subtle indication towards the name of the Promised Messiah, which is *Ḥakam* [Arbiter]. This village was named Islāmpūr Qāḍī Mājhī at the time of King Bābar, when a large area of the region of Mājh was conferred upon my ancestors to govern. Gradually, this rule became a self-governing State, and due to common usage, the word '*Qāḍī*' changed into '*Qāḍī*' which later, turned into Qadian. Hence, the words Nazareth and Islāmpūr Qāḍī are most meaningful names. One of them denotes spiritual verdure, while the other infers spiritual arbitration, which was the task of the Promised Messiah. Your Majesty, Empress of India, may God bless your life with honour and happiness. How blessed is your reign. The hand of God supports your objectives from Heaven. Angels are beautifying the pathways of your benevolence for your subjects and your good intention. The exquisite vapours of your justice are rising like clouds so that they might turn the entire country into the envy of springtime. Mischievous is such a person who does not value your reign and wretched is the one who is not grateful for your favours. Since it is a matter of certainty that there is affinity between hearts, I have no need to employ verbosity in order to express that I have sincere affection for you and in particular there is love and high regard for you in my heart. Our prayers for you continue night and day in the likeness of flowing water. We are not your subjects due to harsh political pressures. Rather, our hearts are drawn towards you because of your countless qualities. O auspicious Queen of India! Blessed be your greatness and good-name. God watches over the country that you oversee. The hand of God's mercy rests upon the subjects of whom you are a guardian. Moved by your pure intentions, God has sent me so that I may once again establish the ways of virtue, pure morals and reconciliation. Your Majesty, Empress of India, I have been informed by God the Exalted that a fault exists in both Muslims and Christians, which has distanced them from true spiritual life. This fault does not allow the two of them to come together; on the contrary, it is creating mutual discord among them. The fault is that there are two extremely dangerous and utterly erroneous views held by Muslims. They consider Jihad of the sword for the sake of religion as being an article of faith and this obsession leads them to believe that by murdering an innocent person they have done a very good deed. This belief has been corrected to a large extent amongst a majority of the Muslims in British India and the hearts of thousands of Muslims have been cleansed by my efforts which span twenty-two to twenty-three years. However, there is no doubt that in some foreign countries these thoughts are still actively held. It is as if these people have understood violence and compulsion to be the core and essence of Islam. However, this view is absolutely false. The Qur'an clearly commands not to raise the sword in order to spread Islam and that the innate qualities of the religion should be presented and that others should be attracted through pious models. Do not think that in the early days of Islam use of the sword was commanded, because the sword was never wielded to spread religion. Quite the contrary, it was drawn in self-defence against enemy attacks or in order to establish peace. Compulsion in faith was never the objective. It is a pity that this fault still exists among wrongdoing Muslims. For their reformation, I have distributed an excess of fifty thousand short and detailed books and leaflets in quantity, throughout the country and abroad. I am hopeful that soon a time shall come when the Muslims will be cleared of this blemish.

The other fault which exists within our Muslim people is that they await a militant Messiah and Mahdi whom they presume will fill the world with blood. This notion is completely false. It is written in our authentic books that neither shall the Promised Messiah engage in war, nor shall he raise the sword. On the contrary, he will possess the essence and character of ʿĪsā [Jesus], on whom be peace, in every respect. He shall be so imbued with his nature that it shall be as if he is exactly the like of him. These two faults are found in the present-day Muslims due to which most of them hold rancour against other nations. However, God has sent me so that I may remove these faults. The title of *Qāḍī* or *Ḥakam*, which has been conferred upon me, is so that I may issue a verdict in this regard.

In comparison to them, an error prevalent amongst the Christians as well is that, God forbid, they hold the word 'curse' to be applicable to someone as holy and revered as the Messiah, who has been called "Light" in the Holy Gospel. They do not understand that *laʿn* [cursing] and *laʿnat* [curse] is a cognate word in Hebrew and Arabic. It signifies that the heart of the cursed person being utterly rebellious, distant and separate from God becomes as defiled and impure as the body is spoiled and ruined with leprosy. Experts in Arabic and Hebrew concur that one can only be called *malʿūn* or *laʿntī* [i.e., accursed] in the case when one's heart severs all ties of love, understanding and obedience to God, and becomes so subservient to Satan as if to become the progeny of Satan. God becomes displeased with him and he becomes weary of God; God becomes his enemy and he becomes an enemy of God; this is why *laʿīn* [i.e., accursed] is a term used for Satan. Therefore, to suggest such a name for the Messiah, on whom be peace, and to forge similarity between his pure and luminous heart, and God forbid, the dark heart of Satan; to assume about one, who according to them [i.e., the Christians], is from God and is an embodiment of light; who is from Heaven; who is the door to knowledge; the pathway of divine understanding and is the inheritor of God; that God forbid, such a one became accursed, or in other words, he was rejected by God; became an enemy of God; his heart became darkened; he turned away from God; became blinded of divine understanding; became an inheritor of Satan and became worthy of the label which is specific to Satan, meaning, 'the accursed,' is such a belief that upon hearing it, the heart crumbles and the body trembles. Did the heart of God's Messiah become as averse to God as the heart of Satan? Was the holy Messiah of God ever confronted with a time when he became displeased with God and actually became an enemy of God? This is a grave mistake and a great disrespect; the heaven might well-nigh burst thereat. In short, the Muslim belief on Jihad is but ill-will towards mankind, while this doctrine of the Christians is ill-will against God Himself. If it is possible that darkness may exist where there is light, then it is also possible that, God forbid, at some point in time, the heart of the Messiah allowed for the lethal state of curse to enter it. If the salvation of humanity depends on such disrespect then it is better that no one attains salvation. For it is better that all sinners die as opposed to declaring a bright and glorious person such as the Messiah as being one who fell into the darkness of ignorance and curse, and into the pit of God's enmity. Hence, I am undertaking efforts to bring about a reformation in the belief of the Muslims as well as in this doctrine of the Christians. I am grateful that God the Exalted granted me success in both these objectives. Since I was accompanied by heavenly signs and divine miracles, I was not confronted with much difficulty in order to convince the Muslims. Having witnessed wondrous and extraordinary Signs of God, thousands of Muslims accepted me. They abandoned the dangerous doctrines that were savagely held in their hearts. [Those who have joined] my community have become sincere well-wishers of this government. I am very pleased that their fervent obedience is of the first order in British India. In order to remove this error of the Christians, God has helped me in such a way that I have no words to express my gratitude. In other words, it has been proven by many conclusive arguments and through solid reasoning that the Messiah, on whom be peace, did not die on the Cross. On the contrary, God saved this innocent Prophet from the Cross. By the grace of God the Exalted, he was interred alive whilst in a state of swoon and not of death. He then emerged from the tomb alive according to his statement in the Gospel that his condition would be similar to that of Prophet Yūnus [Jonah]. His words in the Gospel are that he would show the miracle of Prophet Yūnus. Therefore, he exhibited the miracle of entering the tomb alive and emerging from it alive. These are the facts we discern from the Gospels. In addition to this, we have received the great glad-tiding that it has been established through categorical arguments that the tomb of 'Īsā [Jesus], on whom be peace, is situated in Srinagar, Kashmir. It has been proven that he fled the land of the Jews and arrived to Afghanistan through Naṣībain. For a period in time, he settled at Koh-e-Nuʿmān, after which he settled in Kashmir. He lived to the age of 120 years and died in Srinagar. His tomb is still present in the quarter Khanyār, Srinagar. I have written a book entitled *Masīḥ Hindustān Meiṅ* [Jesus in India] on this subject. This is a great triumph that I have been granted and I know that sooner or later, this will result in two esteemed nations: the Muslims and Christians, who have long been separated, in becoming mutual and close friends. They shall bid farewell to many disputes and will come together in love and friendship. Since this is what has been decreed in Heaven, our British government has also become greatly drawn towards concord between nations as it is evident from various clauses of the 'Sedition Law.' An underlying secret is that any preparation which takes place in the heavens by God the Exalted, is complimented by according thoughts that begin to develop in the heart of worldly government as well. Thus, owing to the good-intention of Her Majesty, God the Exalted has created means by which such unity may be forged between the two nations known as the Christians and Muslims, that hereafter, they should not be considered as being two apart.

Now, hereafter, no reasonable person will believe with respect to the Messiah, on whom be peace, that God forbid, at any time his heart became imbued with the poisonous state of curse, because curse is the result of crucifixion. As such, being crucified is not proven. On the contrary, what is proven is that by virtue of the blessings of his prayers that were offered throughout the night in the Garden [of Gethsemane]; and according to the will of the angel who appeared[*] in the dream of the wife of Pontius Pilate

---

[*]. It is not acceptable in any way and the conscience of any learned person would not accept that while God the Exalted had firmly willed to crucify the Messiah, despite this, His angel anxiously moved here and there to set him free - at times putting love of the Messiah in the heart of Pontius Pilate making him say that he did not find any sin in Christ, and at times appearing in the dream of the wife of Pontius Pilate saying that if Jesus Christ was crucified, misfortune would befall her. How strange is it that an angel should have difference of opinion with God.

to recommend saving the Messiah, on whom be peace; and as per the similitude given by the Messiah himself of Prophet Yūnus [Jonah] surviving in the belly of the fish for three days as an illustration of his own outcome, God the Exalted saved him from the Cross and its result, which was 'curse.' His distressed plea of *'Eli Eli lama sabachthani'* (**) was heard by God. This is clear proof which makes the heart of every seeker after truth jump with joy. Undoubtedly, it is a fruit of the blessings of Her Majesty, the Empress of India, which has cleared the name of the Messiah, on whom be peace, from the unwarranted slander of approximately nineteen hundred years.

I do not consider it appropriate to further prolong this humble submission. I realise that I have not been able to fully convey the degree of enthusiasm I hold at heart to submit my sincerity, loyalty and gratefulness to the Empress of India, may her sovereignty endure. Helpless, I end with the supplication that Allah the Exalted, Who is the Master of the Heaven and the earth and endows a handsome reward for good deeds, may grant good recompense from Heaven to this benefactress, the Empress of India, may her sovereignty endure. May such grace be conferred upon her which is not only limited to this world, rather, bestows her true and eternal prosperity of the Hereafter as well. May God keep her happy and furnish means by which she may receive eternal happiness. May He command His angels to illuminate the heart of the blessed Queen, who is so gracious to humanity, with revelation which instantly descends upon the heart like lightening

---

**. The translation is, 'My God, My God, why hast thou forsaken me?'

and enlightens the whole of it, and brings about an extraordinary change. O Lord, keep our Empress of India forever happy in all respects and may it be so that a higher power from You draws her to Your everlasting light and enters her into [an abode of] eternal and everlasting tranquillity, for nothing is beyond You. Everyone say, *Āmīn!*

Submitted by the humble one,

Mirzā Ghulām Aḥmad
Qadian, District Gurdaspur
The Punjab
20 August 1899

AN IMPORTANT NOTE

Please note that, in this translation, words given in parenthesis ( ) are the words of the Promised Messiah[as]. If any explanatory words or phrases are added by the translator for the purpose of clarification, they are put in square brackets [ ]. Footnotes given by the Publishers are marked [Publishers]. All references, unless otherwise specified, are from the Holy Quran. Biblical references are from the King James version.

The following abbreviations have been used. Readers are urged to recite the full salutations when reading the book:

- sa *ṣallallāhu 'alaihi wa sallam*, meaning 'may the peace and blessings of Allah be upon him' is written after the name of the Holy Prophet Muḥammad[sa].
- as *'alaihis salām*, meaning 'on whom be peace' is written after the name of Prophets other than the Holy Prophet Muḥammad[sa].
- ra *raḍiy-Allāhu 'anhu/'anhā/'anhum*, meaning 'may Allah be pleased with him/her/them' is written after the names of

the Companions of the Holy Prophet Muḥammad[sa] or of the Promised Messiah[as].

aba *ayyadahullāhu Ta'ālā binaṣrihil 'Azīz,* meaning 'may Allah the Almighty help him with his powerful support' is written after the name of the present Head of the Ahmadiyya Muslim Jamā'at, Ḥaḍrat Mirza Masroor Ahmad, Khalīfatul-Masīḥ V[aba].

In transliterating Arabic words we have followed the following system adopted by the Royal Asiatic Society.

| ا | at the beginning of a word, pronounced as *a, i, u* preceded by a very slight aspiration, like *h* in the English word 'honour'.
| ث | *th*, pronounced like *th* in the English word '*thing*'.
| ح | *ḥ*, a guttural aspirate, stronger than *h*.
| خ | *kh*, pronounced like the Scotch *ch* in '*loch*'.
| ذ | *dh*, pronounced like the English *th* in '*that*'.
| ص | *ṣ*, strongly articulated *s*.
| ض | *ḍ*, similar to the English *th* in '*this*'.
| ط | *ṭ*, strongly articulated palatal *t*.
| ظ | *ẓ*, strongly articulated *z*.
| ع | ', a strong guttural, the pronunciation of which must be learnt by the ear.
| غ | *gh*, a sound approached very nearly in the *r* '*grasseye*' in French, and in the German *r*. It requires the muscles of the throat to be in the 'gargling' position whilst pronouncing it.
| ق | *q*, a deep guttural *k* sound.

ع ʾ, a sort of catch in the voice.

Short vowels are represented by:
- *a* for ◌َ (like *u* in '*bud*')
- *i* for ◌ِ (like *i* in '*bid*')
- *u* for ◌ُ (like *oo* in '*wood*')

Long vowels by:
- *ā* for ◌ا or آ (like *a* in '*father*');
- *ī* for ي ◌ِ or ◌ِي (like *ee* in '*deep*');
- *ū* for و ◌ُ (like *oo* in '*root*');

Other:
- *ai* for ي ◌َ (like *i* in '*site*');
- *au* for و ◌َ (resembling *ou* in '*sound*')

The consonants not included in the above list have the same phonetic value as in the principal languages of Europe. Curved commas are used in the system of transliteration, ' for ع , ' for ء.

We have not transliterated Arabic words which have become part of English language, e.g., Islam, Quran, Hadith, Mahdi, jihad, Ramadan, ummah, etc. The Royal Asiatic Society rules of transliteration for names of persons, places and other terms, could not be followed throughout the book as many of the names contain non-Arabic characters and carry a local transliteration and pronunciation style which in itself is also not consistent either.

GLOSSARY

Aḥmadiyya Muslim Jamā'at—The Community of Muslims who have accepted the claims of Ḥaḍrat Mirzā Ghulām Aḥmad[as] of Qadian as the Promised Messiah and Mahdi. The Community was established by Ḥaḍrat Mirzā Ghulām Aḥmad[as] in 1889, and is now under the leadership of his fifth *khalīfah*—Ḥaḍrat Mirza Masroor Ahmad (may Allah be his help). The Community is also known as **Jamā'at-e-Aḥmadiyya**. A member of the Community is called an **Aḥmadī Muslim** or simply an **Aḥmadī**.

Allah—Allah is the personal name of God in Islam. To show proper reverence to Him, Muslims often add *Ta'ālā*, translated here as 'the Exalted', when saying His Holy name.

Al-Imam al-Mahdi—The title given to the Promised Reformer by the Holy Prophet Muḥammad[sa]; it means the guided leader.

Āmīn—May Allah make it so.

Currency values—The booklet uses rupees, anna and paisa. Rupee was the main unit of currency in India, anna is 1/16 of a rupee and paisa is 1/4 of an anna.

Ḥaḍrat—A term of respect used for a person of established righteousness and piety.

Holy Prophet[sa]—A term used exclusively for the Founder of Islam, Ḥaḍrat Muḥammad, may peace and blessings of Allah be upon him.

Holy Quran—The Book sent by Allah for the guidance of mankind. It was revealed word by word to the Holy Prophet Muḥammad[sa] over a period of twenty-three years.

Ḥuḍūr—Your Holiness; His Holiness.

Jihad—The literal meaning of this word is 'striving'. The term is used to mean self-purification as well as religious wars in some instances.

Mahdi—The literal translation of this word is 'the guided one'. This is the title given by the Holy Prophet Muḥammad[sa] to the awaited Reformer of the Latter Days.

Muḥammad—Proper name of the Prophet of Islam.

Maulānā or Maulavī—A Muslim religious cleric.

The Promised Messiah—This term refers to the Founder of the Aḥmadiyya Muslim Jamā'at, Ḥaḍrat Mirzā Ghulām Aḥmad[as] of Qadian. He claimed that he had been sent by Allah in accordance with the prophecies of the Holy Prophet[sa] about the coming of *al-Imam al-Mahdi* (the Guided Leader) and Messiah.

Sūrah—A term in Arabic referring to a chapter of the Holy Quran.

INDEX

Afghanistan 4, 14

Arabic 4

Babar, King 9

Bethlehem 6

British government
  a well-wisher for the Muslims 4
  services rendered by Promised Messiah[as] in support of 4

British India
  community of Promised Messiah[as] is obedient 14
  most inhabitants love their Queen 1

Caesar 8

Christians
  believe in the re-advent of the Messiah 7
  false belief regarding Jesus[as] 12

Chughtā'ī kings 3

Compulsion
  religious, not permitted in Islam 11

Constantinople 4

Curse
  definition of the word 12
  Jesus[as] can never be the subject of 12

Delhi 3

Egypt 4

Elijah 7

Empress, the
  her extraordinary sympathy 8
  her reign was most appropriate for advent of Promised Messiah[as] 7
  high moral standards 1
  prayers in favour of 1, 5, 6, 16

Gethsemane
  prayers of Jesus at, were accepted 15

Gurdaspur 1

Islam
  was never spread by the sword 11

Islāmpūr Qāḍī
  signifies spiritual arbitration 10

Jesus[as] 12
  did not die on the cross 14
  distressed plea of 16
  Promised Messiah[as] in the likeness of 6

Jesus in India. *See Masīḥ Hindustān Meiṅ*

Jihad
  false concept of 11

false notions removed by Promised Messiah[as] 4
John the Baptist 7
Jonah 14
   survived in the belly of the fish 16
   the sign of 14
Kabul 4
Kashmir
   Jesus migrated to 14
Koh-e-Nuʿmān 14
Lahore 1
Madīnah 4
Makkah 4
Masīḥ Hindustāṅ Meiṅ
   book of the Promised Messiah[as] 14
Messiah
   false belief regarding the, is a dishonour to his holy person 13
Mirzā Ghulām Aḥmad. *See Promised Messiah*
Mirzā Ghulām Murtaḍā
   assisted British government during Mutiny of 1857 4
   late father of the Promised Messiah 3
   overjoyed upon the establishment of British rule in India 3
Mirzā Gul Muḥammad
   a wise and virtuous ruler 3
Mughal family
   countless atrocities committed against them during Sikh reign 3
   Promised Messiah[as] was from a noble 3

Mullahs
   ignorant ideologies of, removed by Promised Messiah[as] 5
Muslims
   believe in the re-advent of the Messiah 7
   false belief on the advent of a militant Messiah and Mahdi 11
   have witnessed extraordinary Signs in favour of Promised Messiah 14
Mutiny of 1857 4
Naṣībain 14
Nazareth 6, 8
   signifies spiritual verdure 10
   signifies verdure and freshness 8, 9
Persian 4
Pontius Pilate
   his wife saw a dream 15
Promised Messiah[as] 1
   appointed by God the Exalted 6
   divine claim of the 6
   efforts for the reformation of Muslims and Christians 13
   endowed the title of *Ḥakam* 9, 12
   endowed the title of *Qāḍī* 12
   from a noble Mughal family of the Punjab 3
   great sincerity for Her Majesty 2
   published a quantity of 50,000 writings in support of British government 4
   published writings in Urdu, Persian and Arabic 4

spiritual arbitration was a task of 10

vested with essence and disposition of Jesus[as] 7

Prophecy

regarding the advent of the Promised Messiah[as] 7

Qadian

original name was Islāmpūr Qāḍī Mājhī 9

origins of the word 9

seventy miles northeast from Lahore 1

Queen. *See Empress, the*

Qur'an, the Holy

does not permit violence to spread Islam 11

Satan

one who is subservient to, is accursed 12

the accursed 13

Sedition Law

accord between nations due to the 15

Sikh reign 3

many atrocities committed during, 3

Srinagar

Jesus[as] died in, at age of 120 14

Jesus[as] migrated to 14

Syria 4

Toḥfa-e-Qaiṣariyyah

earlier dispatched to Her Majesty as a gift 2, 5

Urdu 4

www.ingramcontent.com/pod-product-compliance
Lightning Source LLC
Chambersburg PA
CBHW071549080526
44588CB00011B/1842